THE LAST AND BEST OF ALL CREATIONS

WOMAN AS A DIVINE VESSEL IN THE HAND OF GOD

EDITH CHIMA-ORJI

Copyright © 2022 Edith Chima-Orji

All rights reserved. No part of this book may be reproduced, stored, or transmitted by any means—whether auditory, graphic, mechanical, or electronic—without written permission of both publisher and author, except in the case of brief excerpts used in critical articles and reviews. Unauthorized reproduction of any part of this work is illegal and is punishable by law.

This book is a work of non-fiction. Unless otherwise noted, the author and the publisher make no explicit guarantees as to the accuracy of the information contained in this book and in some cases, names of people and places have been altered to protect their privacy.

Scripture taken from the King James Version of the Bible.

ISBN: 979-8-88640-469-2 (sc)
ISBN: 979-8-88640-470-8 (hc)
ISBN: 979-8-88640-471-5 (e)

Because of the dynamic nature of the Internet, any web addresses or links contained in this book may have changed since publication and may no longer be valid. The views expressed in this work are solely those of the author and do not necessarily reflect the views of the publisher, and the publisher hereby disclaims any responsibility for them.

One Galleria Blvd., Suite 1900, Metairie, LA 70001
1-888-421-2397

Many women are not standing in
their places of calling because of fear.
Women should learn, know, and appreciate
their positions in the inclusive plan of
God for humankind.

CONTENTS

Dedication vii
Acknowledgement ix
The Woman of God: Edith Chima-Orji xi
Introduction xiii
Chapter 1   Who is a Divine Woman? 1
Chapter 2   Divine Women in the Bible 7
    Dorcas 9
    Lydia, Lois, and Eunice 11
    Ruth 12
    Jochebed 13
    Abigail 15
    Rahab 16
    Hannah 17
    Esther 19
    Deborah (Judges 4:14) 21
    The Woman with the Issue of Blood (Matthew 9:20–22) 22
Chapter 3   Qualities of a Divine Woman 25
    Love 26
    Peace 29
    Unity 30
    Humility and Obedience 31
    Faithfulness 32
    Patience and Self-Control 33
    Kind and Forgiving 34
    Diligence and Active Service 35
    Devotes Time to Prayer, Fasting, and Bible Study 36

Chapter 4	Woman and the Family	39
Chapter 5	Woman and the Church	43
Chapter 6	Woman as a Leader	49
Chapter 7	The Call of a Woman	55
Chapter 8	Problems	61
Chapter 9	Conclusion	67
Bibliography		71

DEDICATION

I dedicate this book to God Almighty who gave me the inspiration, ideas, wisdom and boldness in writing this book.

I also dedicate this book to my grandmother Fiesta Nelson Nwosu who was a prayer warrior, woman of destiny, and lived a life of emulation. She also brought me up in the ways of the Lord, taught me how to pray and to live a life worthy of emulation.

ACKNOWLEDGEMENT

I thank all whose work, support, research and encouragement helped me in writing this book. I knowledge HRH Eze C. Nelson Nwosu whose ideas were appreciated and used in writing of the script. Mr Uche Nwosu who edited part of the script. My appreciation goes to my families High Chief Chinedu Nwosu, Pastor Uzoma & Pastor Mrs Stella Nwaka, Chief Kinson Nwosu, Mr Charles Nwosu, Mr Henry Nzenwata for their prayers for the success of this book. I also appreciate my lovely mother Roseline Nelson for supporting my book. And my beautiful children Victoria, Eunice and Esther for their sacrifice while I was away in writing this script. I thank Mr Fabian C. Orji who contributed to the writing of this book. I appreciate Evangelist Mabel Omotosho for her support.

My sincere appreciation goes to Andra Jane (Westbow Press) who called excessively with persuasion, her kind words and encouragement, motivated me in publishing my book, even though I don't have money at that time. I acted in faith and worked hard for it. I am glad I did to the glory of God. I will not forget Westbow Press team & Editorial team for editing the book, their patience in working with me and making sure my book was published even though they missed the dateline.

THE WOMAN OF GOD: EDITH CHIMA-ORJI

Edith Chima-Orji is the Founder of International Women of Faith Fellowship (IWOFF). She is a dedicated Christian, hardworking, very accommodating, cheerful, faithful & honest in her work with God. She is a journalist by profession; an ordained pastor, and teacher of the word. She practiced journalism for 15 years in Nigeria, West Africa and later taught English/Media Studies in American International School in Cotonou, Benin Republic, West Africa before going into humanitarian services, the area she was called by God and where her heart is.

She graduated from the University of Lagos and Nigerian Institute of Journalism in 1994 and has PGD in Theology from Redeemed Christian Bible College in 2007. She studied Sociology and Journalism respectively. She is currently doing her BSN (Bachelor of Science in Healthcare Administration) at Dallas Baptist University.

She was brought up in a Christian family. At a very tender age, her life was greatly influenced and shaped by her grandmother. Her grandmother was a devout Christian and this was what she impacted on her children, Edith Chima Orji, being one of them. She learnt under her, the necessity and virtues of good living which include constant prayer, respect, obedience and fear of God through Jesus Christ. Through her grandmother's counsels and guidance, she was patterned and became an opinion moulder and a leader in the Christian and secular circles.

These have made her to steer away from vices, even from pressure among her peers. The grand old lady, now late, also taught her to live a selfless Christian life and this prompted Edith to give her life to Christ in 1986.

Since then God's love, grace and mercy have been upon her life. God has been so good and faithful to her and her family. The Lord gave her a burden to serve the needy and the helpless in Benin Republic, even beyond that West African nation.

Edith has been in ministry (as Children and Adult Pastor) for over 20 years. This Woman of God has served as a volunteer to many ministries, churches and organizations in training and mentoring of both of adults, youths and kids in Africa and in the USA. She continues to create awareness in many other countries that lack the knowledge of God. She has planted churches in Benin Republic of West Africa, Ghana and Nigeria.

She is truly a Godly woman, doing God's work. As a teacher, preacher and interpreter of the WORD, Edith displays rare talent that pictures her as a marvelous story teller, an informed writer, a creative dramatist, an avid reader consummate reporter whose robust encapsulation of national and international events have taken her to many countries including the Republic of South Africa.

This woman of God is a renowned Author. In fact, she has written three books that are yet to be published. She speaks a little French and some African languages. She is blessed with three wonderful children.

INTRODUCTION

Have you ever paused to ask yourself the all-important questions, "Who am I?" "What am I doing here?" "Where do I go from here?" In John 18:37, Jesus answered all three questions with the confidence of a man who knew that he had a date to keep with God.

Jesus knew He was not an accident of birth. Do you? Jesus knew His whole life was to fulfill a divine purpose, a divine destiny, but do you? Do you thank God for who He has made you? Or are you forever wishing you were another person? "To this end was I born" (John 18:37). God made you a woman, a unique creature with a unique personality and unique potential for some specific purposes.

Really, every woman who has lived a fulfilled life as a mother, minister, missionary, or manager of a home has to face these great questions. While Queen Esther trembled, the fate of thousands of Jews in Babylon hung in the balance.

Mordecai's stirring question to her at the dark hour was "Who knoweth whether thou art come to the kingdom for such a time as this" (Esther 4:14 KJV). Her response to that question spurred her on to purposeful actions. And the rest is glorious history of deliverance for her people, the Jews.

Ida Scudder was only a teenager, a missionary's daughter in India, when she had to face the question of life. In one single dreadful night, she witnessed three men approach her home and seek her help—not that of her father, who was a medical doctor—for the lives of their dying wives. Each of them flatly refused male help because of cultural taboos. "Alone in her room, Ida wrestled with the pain, the sorrow, and the rising conviction that if she were a trained doctor, she could have done something." Scudder (1918). But there is nothing I can do," Ida said. Nothing? With three women dying less than a mile away for want of a woman doctor? She struggled with the voice of God all through the night. In the morning, she inquired after the welfare of all three young women; they were all dead. Ida felt she could die too. She fell before God. When she arose, Ida announced to her father and mother, "I'm going to America to study to be a doctor so I can come back and help the women of India." Conviction rang in her voice as she answered the call of God on her life, the purpose of her existence. Before her death, she said, "I feel a great satisfaction because God has been very good to me. God called me and God knows best where a life should be spent. Think about that."

Mary Crowley lost her joy because of her Christian beliefs and her strong faith in God. After the initial shock, she arose with great faith and grim determination to start her own company. She became a multimillionaire, but she never boasted about her riches or wisdom, but in knowing the Lord as her personal Lord and Savior. Her words to women like you and me are very inspiring. "See yourself as an achiever, a queen. Reject the idea that you're handicapped in any way. Imagine yourself as a co-worker with God. Expect that great things are going to happen, and then work to bring them happen."

Mary Slessor was a focused woman whose life dream was to stand up for the cause of Christ in the dark region of Calabar. She knew her calling and followed its course. She left her country in Europe to live as a missionary in Nigeria, Africa, where she stopped the killing of twin babies in southeastern Nigeria.

Whatever your calling as a woman, you will one day come to a moment of truth when you will have to evaluate yourself as to the fulfillment of that calling.

Who is a Divine Woman?

What is divine? Divine means excellent.

> And the LORD God caused a deep sleep to fall upon Adam, and he slept: and he took one of his ribs, and closed up the flesh instead thereof;
>
> And the rib, which the LORD God had taken from man, made he a woman, and brought her unto the man.
>
> And Adam said this is now bone of my bones, and flesh of my flesh: she shall be called Woman, because she was taken out of man. (Genesis 2:21–23)

The woman happens to be a new creature designed and created by God. When God created the heavens and the earth, He spoke them into existence. When God created man, He formed him and breathed life into his nostril. But the woman was fashioned after God had already breathed the breath of life into the man. Hence, the woman is the last and best of all creations. The woman is very important.

Women play important roles in the home. As mothers, they help in the upbringing of their children and in the smooth running of the affairs of the family. Hence, a God-fearing, dedicated, Christian woman is an invaluable asset to her husband and family. A prayerful Christian woman is the neck on which the head of the husband rests and a veritable instrument in the upliftment of the family, church, and community. Throughout the Bible, we found God extending His expectations and roles of women from the home to the church and to the community.

> And the LORD God said, it is not good that the
> man should be alone; I will make him an help meet
> for him. (Genesis 2:18)

Woman must not and cannot claim equality with man because God did not create woman as man's equal. Nor did He make us to be underdogs. God created woman as a helpmeet and companion.

> Wives submit yourselves unto your own husbands,
> as unto the Lord.
>
> For the husband is the head of the wife, even as
> Christ is the head of the church: and he is the Savior
> of the body. (Ephesians 5:22–23)

We are created to attend to our husbands' needs in love and humility, submitting to them.

A woman's submissive or supportive role does not make her less a person, less in honor, or less in potential. Both man and woman, while having different roles in the family and church, are created in the image of God. God never emphasized sexual diversity but sexual unity (Genesis 2:24).

The apostle Paul wrote in Galatians 3:26–28, "You are all sons of God through faith in Christ. For as many as have been baptized into Christ have put on Christ. There is neither Jew nor Greek, there is neither bond nor free, nor female; for you are all one in Christ Jesus."

The apostle Peter also emphasized that men should treat women with understanding and give them honor as the weaker vessels and as heirs together with men of the grace of life, so their prayers may not be hindered. Both man and woman, when they have given their lives to Christ, are regenerated and have equal opportunities to do work for God.

A woman is one who has the fear of God in her life.

- She is a peacemaker and a good adviser.
- She maintains her integrity in the family, church, and society.
- She always obeys her husband.
- She is her husband's helpmeet and recognizes him as the head of the family.
- She knows how to maintain love, peace, and unity in the family.
- She gives top priority to the education and training of her children.
- She has no time for gossip, fault-finding, or destructive criticism.
- She loves to study and preach the Word of God.
- She is sure of her salvation.
- She is honest in her business.
- She has no time for worldly competition.
- She has a forgiving spirit.
- She is kind and hospitable.
- She is always active in the things of God.
- She observes her quiet time.
- She is attractive to her husband and presentable to her children.
- She does not rob God of money, time, or talent.
- She is not a hypocrite.
- She satisfies her husband in all good things.
- She knows how to entertain and welcome visitors at home, in church, and in society.
- She keeps her family secrets.

- She is a prayer warrior.
- She is kind to the poor, generous to those around her, a loving mother, faithful in small duties, and humble before God.
- She is a teacher of good things.
- She shows all good fidelity and adorns the doctrine of God.
- She is pure and holy.
- She does not put her children ahead of her husband.
- She is diligent and dependable.

Divine Women in the Bible

The Bible is replete with women of faith who, one way or the other, made history and helped to shape our contemporary Christian faith and beliefs. Thus, Sarah (Genesis 25:21), Rachael (Genesis 29:31; 30:1), Manoah's wife (Judges 13), Hannah (1 Samuel 1), the Shunamite woman (2 Kings 4:14), and Elizabeth (Luke 1) had their breakthroughs through faith, love, and sobriety. Through their strong faith, these women moved the hand of God.

Deborah, Abigail, Huldah, Esther, and the daughters of Zelophehad are examples of women who knew how and when to assert themselves in a godly way and do exploits.

The Bible shows that women can lead, be strong, and assert authority. There are the likes of Mary and Martha, who ministered to the needs of our Lord Jesus. Joanna and Susanna provided for Christ from their substance (Luke 8:3). Priscilla, together with her husband, preached the gospel, used their home as a discipleship school and a church, and bore the burdens of apostle Paul.

DORCAS

Dorcas's works of charity made people weep bitterly at her death until she was brought back to life (Acts 9:36–47). She was a benevolent woman who devoted herself to lovingly helping others. She was mentioned in the Bible because of her benevolent nature.

As Christlike women, we should engage in good works and deeds that uplift and encourage other people. The character and work of Dorcas are typical of the influence of Christianity in the world, differentiating it from all other religions—caring for the weak and poor, lifting up women, and encouraging the weary-minded.

Dorcas was a true disciple of the Lord. Her ministry of giving, especially to widows, was an excellent testimony of the work of grace in her. This woman distributed to the necessity of the saints and was given to hospitality (Romans 12:13). This means that her hospitality was born out of her love for God, not just a routine expenditure. God does not reward His people according to the magnitude of their gifts but according to their motives and faithfulness in ministry and service (1 Corinthians 4:1–2).

Her restoration to life by Peter confirmed God's faithfulness and compassion. It is always good to remember that God is a rewarder of those who diligently seek Him. The Lord keeps records of our daily service to Him, and it is certain that we shall all give accounts of our stewardship at the due time.

Dorcas's work lived after her and had a good report from the church. What about you? Many, instead of giving to the Lord in gratitude for His grace and love, steal from Him and are cursed like Judas Iscariot.

LYDIA, LOIS, AND EUNICE

Lydia was a successful businesswoman, dedicated Christian, and evangelist who helped supply the needs of the ministers of God (Acts 16:14–15).

Lois and Eunice, Timothy's mother and grandmother, respectively, stand out as examples to Christian mothers of proper childcare and training (2 Timothy 1:5).

RUTH

As we know from the biblical book of Ruth, she was a young widow who demonstrated her love and devotion to her mother-in-law, Naomi. She was a kind person noticed by Naomi and Boaz. Ruth was a faithful and dependable wife, the type who would stick with a man in his time of need. She was a woman of true love and humble, responsible, and selfless. She was hardworking and obedient, and she maintained her integrity even in a foreign land. Ruth was loyal to her immediate and extended families. She had the submissive spirit expected of a virtuous woman. By her marriage, Ruth came into the linage of the Messiah, Lord Jesus.

Ruth's character epitomized the qualities of a true, dedicated, Christian woman. In today's society—where there are marital problems, divorces, and social upheavals—the Christian woman should emulate and embrace the sterling qualities of Ruth.

JOCHEBED

A mother can do nothing higher than instill her wisdom, faith, and character into her children. Jochebed did that in the lives of her children.

Jochebed was an authentic woman of God, balanced, mature, self-controlled. She made full creative use of her imagination as well as her practical mind when she did not stop her prayer to God to save her baby, Moses. She was poised even in the face of tragedy. She was able to quiet her inner turmoil and think clearly. Her emotions ran deep, but she was not a victim of those emotions. God was her Master.

There is always something you can do if God is on your side: "all things are possible" (Matthew 19:26). Jochebed took a chance. She could have been killed, and if she had been, she would have had the satisfaction of knowing she tried. Being paralyzed with fear does no one any good, especially in the face of something or someone as evil as this pharaoh.

The baby Jochebed placed in the basket was Moses. And when Pharaoh's daughter found the baby, she took compassion on him and adopted him as her own. She chose his mother to nurse the baby.

Jochebed's compassion moved her to do something instead of nothing, and her baby was saved. God places opportunities for compassion in front of us every day. Whether we recognize or ignore them is up to us.

A woman under God's control is a woman living her life to its highest and fullest. A woman who places her mind in the things of the world will always suffer for it. Take for instance Lot's wife. Literally, she lived for the things of the world—money, expensive gowns, lavish furniture, a big home, too much food and wine. A woman who refused all attempts to save herself from destruction, she clung willfully and stubbornly to her self-centered interests.

Destruction comes to us when we remain chained to our past, no matter what characterized it. If we have lived a selfish, obviously sinful life, it is quite simple to see the error in clinging to our old habits and thought patterns. It takes no great mental revolving to see the futility of holding on to a way of life that brought so much sorrow.

ABIGAIL

She was a capable woman who turned away the wrath of a warrior (1 Sam 25:3–19).

Abigail was a woman full of wisdom. She was the best thing that happened in the life of Nabal. When her family was to be wiped out by David as a result of Nabal's inconsiderate, selfish, and foolish disposition toward David, she employed wisdom to avert the danger that was looming over Nabal and saved a whole family from destruction.

Like Abigail, you can utilize your skills and talents to promote peace among feuding brethren. Many husbands have found themselves facing trouble because of the carnal advice of their wives.

God Himself wants to provide us with escape to freedom from grief, hurt feelings, disillusionment, and trouble of any kind. But because He has created us with free wills, as He created Lot's wife, we can block Him by securing the chains of our past lives with our own hands.

RAHAB

God is always in motion, working with us where we are and as we are. He trusts His own power to change us day by day into His image. He did not come to condemn anybody. He came to save us as He saved Rahab and her family. He does not wait for us to become perfect and in possession of high, pure thoughts and unmixed motives before He moves through us. No human being is ever truly ready to be an instrument of God. He waits only for the sign of faith that was so evident in this woman, Rahab, and then He begins to move in His redemptive power.

Rahab knew, recognized and confessed the identity and the power of the God of Israel, and she was saved (Hebrews 11:31; James 2:25).

We are told she married Salmon and so, became a Hebrew. She was the mother of Boaz, who married Ruth, whose son was Jesse, the father of David, through whose life Jesus was born (Matthew 1:5).

HANNAH

Hannah was an ideal mother (1 Samuel 1:20; 2:19). Hannah asked for one child but had five extra (1 Samuel 2:21).

Who was Hannah? She was a prayer warrior. She prayed until God heard.

She was a covenant partner with God, and she kept her covenant with God.

She was a grateful woman.

Another quality of Hannah's is self-denial. After the baby came, she gave God the glory (2 Samuel 2:1–2). She lived a life of holiness and purity.

We need to cultivate Hannah's prayerful style: not giving up, hoping, trusting, and believing God to answer at the appointed time.

Hannah's prayers teach us that whatever we have or receive is on loan from God because all good gifts are from above. Unlike many mothers who had to wait a while to receive a child from the Lord, Hannah paid her vow and wholeheartedly followed through on her promise to dedicate little Samuel to God and His service as soon as possible.

This is what is required from all godly parents, to let go freely of their children for God's use. Like the eagles, we must gradually let go of our children so that they can mature, grow into the grace of God, and fulfill their divine destinies like Samuel. Being overprotective or overbearing parents will do them more harm than good in later years.

Hannah was also exceedingly thankful (1 Samuel 2:1–10). We must always be thankful to God for everything. Being stingy with our thanksgiving will only get us into trouble.

A woman is expected to have a devotional spirit to her God and to her husband. This was portrayed by Hannah's steadfastness in looking unto

God for the fruit of the womb and Esther's decision to stand up for her people.

ESTHER

Esther was the woman of great courage. God worked with and through her. Women then and today are being called on by the Lord God to show this kind of courage. God supplied Esther with His wisdom in the high places, just as He is eager to supply us in our times of need.

Esther was beautiful. In spite of that, she refused to be corrupted in a corrupt society. She maintained her virginity in a sexually immoral environment (Esther 2:2, 8, 17).

She found favor with God and her keepers. She sacrificed her life for her people. Esther helped the Jews to enjoy rest from their enemies (Esther 9:17) according to God's promise to His people.

She was open to advice and willing to act. She exhibited godly wisdom by seeking the face of God in prayer and fasting in times of trouble. In calling for a fast before she went to the king, Esther put her case completely into God's hand (Esther 4:16). She remarked, "I will go to the king which is against the law; and if I perish, I perish."

She used her divine endowment as a woman in making demands from her husband. Esther was a woman of wisdom. This is shown in the manner she presented her petition and request before the king. She won victory for her people and saved many lives.

Wherever God can find faith and obedience, He is moved into action to favor and fight the battle of His people. It is a good Christian virtue to always trust in the Lord, even in the face of impossible situations. The story of Esther shows the inelastic power of God to save, deliver, and bless.

DEBORAH (JUDGES 4:14)

She was a patriotic woman who desired a change for her people. She contributed her quota to ensure that change manifested.

Deborah was a judge and prophetess. She accompanied Barak into battle to deliver the children of Israel. She was a source of inspiration. Deborah played the supportive role expected of a godly woman.

THE WOMAN WITH THE ISSUE OF BLOOD (MATTHEW 9:20-22)

We see few principles demonstrated by this woman who, out of desperation, exhibited violent faith that brought her healing. Women have a great many lessons to learn from this woman of faith (Luke 8:48).

Despite spending all her life's resources notwithstanding, she grew worse., This poor woman kept looking for a cure for this seemingly incurable condition.

The woman said to herself, "if I may but touch the hem of his garment, I shall be whole" (Matthew 9:21). She kept seeking in spite of several disappointments from physicians (Mark 5:26; Luke 8:43). Let's learn a great lesson from this woman. There is always one resource remaining to be tried: the unfailing power of the Lord Jesus Christ. The arm of flesh will not only fail us, but it will also bring untold hardship and frustration (Jeremiah 17:5–6).

The woman faithfully admitted she was the "culprit." She declared before the crowd who she was and how she got her miracle. She was not ashamed to confess the power of Jesus publicly. What about you? Will you hide the goodness of God?

God knows more clearly than we do that we are all faced with situations that require wisdom. Any woman who knows God has access to His wisdom at any time and under any circumstances. Her part is to keep her emotions under control and her mind open to His—God's—wisdom, which He is always eager to give.

God in His wisdom refuses no one who responds to Him in faith. Women like Deborah (Judges 4:14), Hannah, Ruth, and Abigail all have outstanding records worthy of emulation in the Bible.

God did not create the woman out of a whim. Nor did He create her out of error. And He did not plant all the talents, qualities, and abilities in her for naught. Woman was created because she is and will forever be an important and a necessary aspect of man.

Sisters, we cannot let God down. We must play our parts—that is, as the important and necessary aspect of man—with all humility and purposive actions.

We must always remember that we are the one who brings God's favor to man and makes him whole. Man is your head, and one must be submissive to the head so that God's purpose for our lives will be done.

Now that we have seen what those before us have done, what do we want to do about our lives? Are you measuring up to these women in any way? Do you realize that there is a race on, and very few are going to obtain a prize? Why don't you check your lives in reference to the following highlights, and see how well you are doing right now.

Patience, gentleness, love, peace, joy, faith, and everything else that women of note in the Bible have demonstrated are also required of women outside the Bible.

May the Holy Spirit fall on each and every woman believer to make us all good examples and salt of the earth, seasonings, to complement the lives of our families, churches, neighborhoods, and communities. Amen.

Qualities of a Divine Woman

LOVE

Let brotherly love continue.

> Be not forgetful to entertain strangers: for thereby some have entertained angels unawares.
>
> Remember them that are in bonds, as bound with them: and them which suffer adversity, as being yourselves also in the body. (Hebrews 13:1–3)
>
> Beloved, let us love one another: for love is of God; and every one that loveth is born of God, and knoweth God.
>
> He that loveth not knoweth not God; for God is love.
>
> In this was manifested the love of God sent his only begotten Son into the world, that we mighty live through Him. (1 John 4:7– 9)
>
> We know that we have passed from death unto life, because we love the brethren.
>
> He that loveth not his brother abideth in death. (1 John 3:14)
>
> The LORD hath appeared of old unto me, saying, Yea, I have Loved thee with an everlasting love:

therefore with loving- Kind-ness have I drawn thee. (Jeremiah 31:3)

This is my commandment, that ye love one another, as I have loved you.

Greater love hath no man than this, that a man lay down his life for his friends.

Ye are my friends, if ye do whatever I command you. Henceforth I call you not servants; for the servant knoweth not what his lord doeth: but I have called you friends; for all things that I have heard of my Father I have made known unto you.

Ye have not chosen me, but I have chosen you, and ordained you, that ye should go and bring forth fruit, and that your fruit should remain: that whatsoever ye shall ask of the Father in my name, he may give it you.

These things I command you, that ye love one another. (John 15:12–17)

Though I speak with the tongues of men and of angels, and have not charity, I am become as sounding brass, or a tinkling cymbal.

And though I have the gift of prophecy, and understand all mysteries, and all knowledge; and though I have all faith, so that I could remove mountains, and have not charity, I am nothing.

And though I bestow all my goods to feed the poor; and though I give my body to be burned, and have not charity, it profiteth me nothing.

And now abideth faith, hope, charity, these three; but the greatest of these is charity. (1 Corinthians 13:1–3, 13)

What Is Love?

Love is defined as a powerful emotion felt for another, manifesting itself in deep affection or devotion to another person.

A woman is an embodiment of love to everyone around her. Love is about giving and forgiving. Love is a powerful instrument that places you where God will promote you. A Christian woman is a great blessing to her husband, children, neighbors, colleagues at work, customers in business, and even to strangers. We should love with all our hearts, souls, and minds.

When the love of Christ is in your heart, you can give it out to others. You cannot give what you don't have.

Women of God should go all out and use their lives to spell love. Your quality of love is dependent on your level of godliness or how much of you is yielded to God's holy nature of love. God wants to love someone through you. He wants to share His hope, faith, and love with your neighbor, but not without you.

Just as He needed Jesus to give His love to the world, He needs you to share the same love with others near you through your words, life, and actions.

PEACE

> Let us therefore follow after the things which make for peace, and things wherewith one may edify another. (Romans 14:19)
>
> Follow peace with all men and holiness, without which no man shall see the Lord. (Hebrews 12:14)
>
> And seek the peace of the city whither I have caused you to be carried away captives, and pray unto the LORD for it: for in the peace thereof shall ye have peace. (Jeremiah 29:7)

A Christian woman sees it as her responsibility to keep the peace. For the sake of peace, she let's go that which is her right. She frowns at anything that has the tendency to breach the peace in the family, church, and society. She always goes for the things that make for peace. And she tries as much as possible to be at peace with everyone.

UNITY

> Behold, how good and how pleasant it is for brethren to dwell together in unity. (Psalm 133:1)
>
> Endeavouring to keep the unity of the spirit in the bond of peace. (Ephesians 4:3)

A woman understands that unity is the bedrock of strength. She supports ideas that will bring unity to any group to which she belongs. She is always happy when she sees that brethren dwell together in unity. She endeavors to keep the unity of the spirit in the bond of peace.

HUMILITY AND OBEDIENCE

> But he giveth more grace, wherefore he saith, God resisteth the proud, but giveth grace unto the humble. (James 4:6)

> Likewise, ye younger, submit yourselves unto the elder, yea, all of you be subject one to another, and be clothed with humility; for God resisteth the proud, and giveth grace to the humble.

> Humble yourselves therefore under the mighty hand of God, that He may exalt you in due time. (1 Peter 5:5–6)

A Christian woman makes humility and obedience part of her ideal goals in life. Her beauty, academic qualifications, or social status does not make her arrogant. Instead, she humbles herself, knowing very well that "God resisteth the proud, but giveth grace unto the humble."

Humility and obedience make her see her husband as "Lord" (1 Peter 3:6).

She is always ready to obey him in all good things (Ephesians 5:24).

She extends the same mark of respect to constituted authorities, both spiritual and physical (1 Peter 2:17; Titus 3:1–2).

FAITHFULNESS

I have not hid thy righteousness within my heart; I have declared thy faithfulness and thy salvation: I have not concealed thy loving-kindness and thy truth from the great congregation. (Psalm 40:10)

Thy faithfulness is unto all generations: thou hast established the earth, and it abideth. (Psalm 119:90)

O LORD, thou art my God; I will exalt thee, I will praise thy name; for thou hast done wonderful things; thy counsels of old are faithfulness and truth. (Isaiah 25:1)

Faithfulness means loyalty, dedication, and commitment. It's an obligation on every woman of God to be faithful. One of the basic requirements of Christianity is faithfulness. A Christian woman should be faithful to God and her husband. Faithfulness goes with discipline. No investment in faithfulness will go unrewarded.

PATIENCE AND SELF-CONTROL

Now the God of patience and consolation grant you to be like-minded one toward another according to Christ Jesus. (Romans 15:5)

But that on the good ground are they, which in an honest and good heart, having heard the word, keep it, and bring forth fruit with patience. (Luke 8:15)

Remembering without ceasing your work of faith, and labour of love, and patience of hope in our Lord Jesus Christ, in the sight of God and our Father. (1 Thessalonians 1:3)

Knowing this, that the trying of your faith worketh patience.

But let patience have her perfect work, that ye may be perfect and entire, wanting nothing. (James 1:3–4)

A Christian woman is patient while passing through the storms of life. She is joyful in tribulation and relaxed in times of adversity. She does not quarrel or lose her temper when maltreated by others. She keeps her emotions under control and leaves vengeance to God of injustice. In times of need, she quietly waits on the Lord, casting all her cares on Him for He cares for His children (1 Peter 5:7).

KIND AND FORGIVING

And be ye kind one to another, tender-hearted, forgiving one another, even as God for Christ's sake hath forgiven you. (Ephesians 4:32)

Forbearing one another, and forgiving one another, if any man have a quarrel against any: even as Christ forgave you, so also do ye. (Colossians 3:13)

A godly woman learns how to forgive. She is kind and forgiving, and she does not keep malice against anything or anyone. When there is problem, she tries to settle the problem amicably.

DILIGENCE AND ACTIVE SERVICE

> The slothful man roasteth not that which he took in hunting; but the substance of a diligent man is precious. (Proverbs 12:27)

> He becometh poor that dealeth with a slack hand: but the hand of the diligent maketh rich. (Proverbs 10:4)

The godly woman takes part in any program organized by the church for the spiritual growth of its members. She does not waste time that can be used for evangelism, Bible study, fellowship meetings, and so on as she is eager to win souls to God. She is not slothful in business. Through her hard work, she provides for her family, helps the needy, and actively supports the work of God.

DEVOTES TIME TO PRAYER, FASTING, AND BIBLE STUDY

> But we will give ourselves continually to prayer, and to the ministry of the word. (Acts 6:4)

> Be careful for nothing; but in every thing by prayer and supplication with thanksgiving let your requests be made known unto God. (Philippians 4:6)

> For it is sanctified by the word of God and prayer. (1 Timothy 4:5)

Prayer is the expression of the desires of the heart. Prayer is worship, and prayer is praise and thanksgiving. But prayer is primarily asking God for what we need.

The Bible is our spiritual bankbook. Our prayers are the checks we write, drawing on God's infinite resources.

The Bible contains many prayer promises, but I would like us to consider just one: "If ye abide in me, and my words abide in you, ye shall ask what ye will, and it shall be done unto you" (John 15:7). There are three factors involved: abiding, asking, and answering.

Jesus uses the word "abide." His illustration is that of a vine and its branches. The branches are united to the vine and draw upon its life and strength. All the branch has to do is abide, stay in contact with the vine, and it will bear fruit. You and I, as divine women, are united by Christ to the faith. But along with this union, there must be communion; we must fellowship with Christ and draw upon His life and power.

To abide in Christ simply means to keep in fellowship with Him. This we do through the Word of God, worship, and obedience. If we disobey Him, we break the fellowship, and we cannot pray. But if we obey Him and allow His Word to control our lives, we can pray and God will answer. One of the secrets of answered prayer is abiding in the Word and letting the Word abide in you. Spending time in reading the Bible is like spending time conversing with a dear friend.

The prayer life of a Christian woman is a challenge to others. She maintains an effective prayer life and helps build the family altar. She observes a regular quiet time in the presence of the Lord. She doesn't absent herself from church or prayer meetings, or from fasting under a false pretense of ill-health. She observes a regular time of personal and family Bible study. Her prayer life and ability to study God's Word enable her to exhibit good qualities that show loyalty and fondness to God.

Woman and the Family

God has divinely appointed the husband to be the one who makes or takes the final decision on matters within the family. Many do seek the advice of their wives, especially if the husband is not well informed on the issue. When the man makes a decision, his wife should gratefully submit to his God-appointed decision-making authority.

The woman is expected to fulfill her role as a wife to her husband, mother to her children, and as a homemaker. She should mind what she says about her husband and children. She must submit in all things and in reverence of her husband (Ephesians 5:22–24; Colossians 3:18). And she must love her husband (Titus 2:4; Proverbs 31:26).

A Christian woman should apply wisdom in talking to her husband and in terms of taking decisions as well. She sees her prayer as a necessary weapon rather than as an argument. She should learn to satisfy her children spiritually, emotionally, and physically. Love and control are the instruments required in bringing up children.

A divine woman as a homemaker sees to the general welfare of family members. She keeps the home clean (Titus 2:5; Proverbs 31:27).

After marriage, some women become careless about themselves and their homes. They don't take proper care of their bodies, and their dressing becomes poor. Some cannot sweep and clean their houses properly. When you visit some homes unannounced, the whole place will smell bad. Men find this objectionable.

Women should look neat and dress modestly. Modesty is a precept good for us. I don't appreciate it when women, especially married women, dress immodestly, such as wearing tight clothing with low-cut necklines. Each husband should help his wife to wear appropriate clothing rather than having legalistic clothing rules. Young women should be advised as well on their dress (1 Timothy 2:9).

A godly woman prepares good food for her household (Proverbs 31:15). Learn to prepare your husband's favorite food well. And when he is annoyed or stressed, use it to make him happy.

A Christian woman must be hospitable (Hebrews 13:1–3).

Your home is what you make it to be. A Christian commits her problems into the hand of God because He is the originator of marriage. She should also avoid discussing her marriage or the problems in her home to outsiders or questionable friends. When you are under pressure, remain calm. Don't react foolishly when you are passing through trials and temptations.

How well do you listen to your children? Listening involves more than our ears. Your children need your full and undivided attention. By doing so, you will discover any lapses and lacks in the lives of your children, and that will help you to correct matters of concern and know the areas where you can focus your prayers.

Mothers should not abuse their positions. Remember that when it comes to our children, we have a position of power. If we misuse this power, we may never regain our children's trust. And without their trust, it doesn't matter how much charisma we have; we won't have much influence in their lives. When you abuse your position as a mother, you damage your relationship with your children. But worse than that, they endanger their souls.

A divine woman has a place as wife and mother. She has found her mission to help, her necessity to suffer. She understands that her husband is a special gift from God. He was given to her to enrich her life. You are his helpmeet. If you keep complaining and grumbling, how can you fulfill your role as the helpmeet?

As a wife, woman is more than a mate. She is a partner with her husband in their mutual quest for earthly and heavenly goals through separate roles. A subordinate and dutiful wife deserves love and kind treatment from her

husband (Ephesians 5:25–33; Colossians 3:19; 1 Peter 3:7). Acquila and Priscilla are a noble biblical example of a husband-wife team worthy of contemporary emulation. Today, we have Pastor and Pastor Mrs. Adeboye, Pastor Kenneth Hagin, and other great men and women of God we should emulate as well.

At home, some women have no time to teach their children. Some are more concerned with their careers and neglect the spiritual and moral upbringing of their children. They often shift that duty to their maids or teachers at school.

Woman and the Church

The role of the man is leadership, while the woman's role is as a source of strength and support.

The Bible has done more for the elevation of the role of women than any other book or movement. It is necessary to allow and encourage the full participation of women in the ministry and to rightfully ordain them for service in the church.

God never hesitated to use godly women when necessary to achieve His purpose. Many women have been given gifts of administration, teaching, and preaching that should be used in the body of Christ as God leads them.

Luke records the accounts of Mary and Elizabeth. He also tells of Anna the prophetess, who was in the temple when Jesus was brought there as a baby. She was one of the two people who recognized Jesus as the Messiah because of her sensitivity to the Holy Spirit (Luke 2:25–38). We also learn of the widow of Nain and Mary Magdalene—the sinful woman who anointed Jesus's feet (Matthew 26:10)—Joanna and Susanna (Luke 8:3), and Martha and her sister Mary, the widow who gave all she had to God. You can read these chapters for more understanding (Luke chapters 1, 2, 7, 8, 10, 13, and 21). Even in the book of Acts, which records the history of the early church, women are mentioned time and again. Philip, one of the seven deacons, is said to have four daughters who prophesied (Acts 21:8–9).

Women prophesy, teach, preach God's Word, and are filled with the Holy Spirit. Anyone who prophesies can teach everyone in the body of Christ. There is no gender specification on the gifts of prophecy or the Holy Spirit (Acts 2:18; 1 Corinthians 12:8–11). For believers, the Holy Spirit is poured out on men and women alike (Joel 2:29).

Women today are in the ministry. They are servants in the church/ministry as deaconesses and elders in the church community. They have been the backbone of virtually all Christian churches, Christian communities, and missionary work around the world. These ministries are available for both single and married woman throughout Christendom and in almost all denominations. They are great worshippers.

Well-known Redeemed Christian Church of God missionaries include Pastor (Mrs.) Folu Adeboye (Mummy GO, as popularly known and called), and Miss Alma Rohm from Southern Baptist Church USA. Pastor (Mrs.) Adeboye is a woman of integrity and a role model in various areas. She oversees Africa Missions, an arm of the church she founded some years ago. This woman of God has so much passion for lost souls. She is a woman full of compassion, humility, concern, charisma, status, and dedication to God and humankind.

Miss Alma Rohn felt God calling her to be a single-woman missionary teacher in Africa. Alma served as a teacher at a Baptist teacher-training college in Iwo, in southwestern Nigeria. She taught English literature, education, and organ classes. She also served as school librarian, played the piano for the church, led the choir, and so on. She served for fifty-four years in Nigeria. In 1982, King S. O. Abimola II bestowed an African chieftaincy title on her, recognizing her as "Iya Nisin Ilu" ("mother in service of the whole community"). She made a powerful contribution to the nation and her community before she returned to Richmond, Virginia, in September 2004.

Another inspirational person is a businesswoman named Lydia. She accepted the gospel message from Paul and Silas and played a significant part in the growth of the church.

Women, as helpmeets, play complementary roles to men. As such, women should be actively involved in every activity in the church. Each woman has a ministry in the church into which she is called. This could be the same one as the Shunamite woman who ministered to the needs of Prophet Elisha was called and blessed (2 Kings 4:8–11).

It could also be ministry of kindness to the poor or the needy. There is the need for us to enrich the lives of people who are less privileged than us. Proverbs 31:20 says, "she stretcheth out her hand to the poor; yea, she reacheth forth her hands to the needy." Women can be involved in the ministry of Christ's comfort. They can contribute to Christ's comfort today by leading people to Him, by following up on them, and by encouraging their faith in Christ Jesus. They can also contribute to Christ's comfort by ensuring that they are constantly in tune with the Holy Spirit and teaching their children to do same by bringing them up in a godly manner (Matthew 27:55–56).

Women can also feature in the ministry of service. Service comes in various forms and classes, and one needs to identify in which area she can operate effectively. The service could be in intercessory prayer, counseling, choir, evangelism, and visitation. Some of the works women may do are writing Bible class materials and cleaning the church building. I remember when I used to sweep and clean the Church of God every Saturday as a youth. My grandmother gave a prayer point I used to pray as I did that: "Father, as I am sweeping Your house, sweep away my problems." She further told me that when you are working for God, He will work for you.

Each time our pastors entered the church and saw me sweeping and cleaning the church, they prayed for me. And this made a tremendous impact in my life, academics, and ministry.

God equipped women with special caring abilities. These qualities could be employed in the church ministry of caring. Those who are led to care for the aged, teenagers, and motherless babies should heed the call. Care for the people around you with a smile, the right word, a nod of encouragement, listening, and so on.

Woman as a Leader

Who is a leader?

A leader is the person who is ultimately responsible for everything that happens in the organization.

A leader knows where he or she is going and is able to persuade others to follow (Hebrews 13:7–8). The leader is a person who stands out among the followers and, thereby, leads them.

No matter how strong, an organization that tries to succeed without an effective leader will soon crumble. That organization will not achieve its potential for high standards without strong leadership. Not only is it important that our leaders have strong leadership skills, their leadership must be executed in a positive way with lots of encouragement, support, and concrete direction. We can see these characteristics in the Redeemed Christian Church of God today. Good leaders are made, not born. If you have the desire and willpower, you can become an effective leader. Good leadership is developed through hard work involving self-study, education, training, and experience. Good leaders inspire followers.

Divine women as leaders know how to inspire those who work with them to higher goals and greater productivity. They also share their leadership positions over their children. As a mother, you lead your children in every aspect of their lives, including their spiritual well-beings. You can't lead them spiritually without a spiritual leader of your own.

Divine woman as a leader must have good character (Proverbs 31:10–12). Character is what defines us as a person. Leaders who have strong moral character withstand the test of time. You can be easily assessed through examining your character. That is, if you are a person of dubious character, there is no way your life can make others come to Christ. Your character can promote or demote you. We learn from our environment and the types of homes in which we grew up. The ultimate source of truth is God, and the best place to learn about character building is in the Bible.

The virtuous woman is another powerful example of leadership with integrity. Families who support and help each other are much stronger than those where everyone does his or her own thing.

A divine woman is compassionate (Proverbs 31:20). Leaders think of others. If we fail to show compassion for others, how can we expect our children to be compassionate?

She is competent (Proverbs 31:21–25).

She is a communicator (Proverbs 31:26). Effective women leaders need to control their tongues and improve their communication skills. We need to learn to speak with wisdom and faithful instruction.

She has charisma (Proverbs 31:13, 17).

She is God-centered (Proverbs 31:30–31). A woman who fears God is to be praised. "Feared" means to respect, trust, and hope.

The most important factor in leading is our spiritual commitments to God and our faith in Jesus Christ.

The divine woman stands up for what is right. Esther (7:10) is a good example. Doing the right thing isn't always easy under the best circumstances, but doing the right thing under adverse circumstances is a true test of character.

Divine woman must be honest. It is important to speak the truth, even when it hurts.

She must be humble. Humility is an extremely important quality of positive leadership. Jesus Christ is our example to follow. God showed us what the power of love can do by giving His Son, Jesus, to die for our sins (John 3:16).

As divine vessels in the hand of God, we can plug into that power source. Learn to lead with love. Love is the most essential ingredient to motherhood, and it should be the basis for everything we do. If we lead with love, we do not take pleasure in evil or in others' mistakes, but we rejoice in the truth and in those who do God's will.

A divine woman should learn to lead with patience and to be kind. She should not be rude, including when we lead others. Jesus wasn't rude or angry. His actions were not self-seeking; they were selfless.

As a divine woman leader, you should not run away from leading. No matter how tired, discouraged, or down we get, we can't give up because giving up is failure. We have to stay in the race and fix our eyes on Jesus, the author and finisher of our faith (Hebrews 12:1-3). Love never fails because it never gives up.

As a leader, you should eliminate the fear factor. Leaders who have God on their side have nothing to fear. To be competent, we can't be afraid of making mistakes. If we seek God's will when it comes to making decisions. He will lead us, and we don't have to be afraid. When the fear factor threatens you, read His words—God's words—and ask Him for strength (2 Timothy 1:7).

Deborah was a prophetess and one of the great leaders mentioned in the Bible. The story of her life shows how God can accomplish great things through people who are willing to be led by Him. We can have the same courage in parenting that Deborah had on the battlefield if we are willing to listen to God's commandments the way Deborah did.

Phoebe was a deaconess of the church in Cenchrea. She was beloved by Paul and many other Christians for the help she gave them. She filled an important position of leadership (Romans 16:1-2).

Though there were other women mentioned in the Bible who held positions of leadership—such as prophetesses, evangelists, and judges—the previous references, together with the activities of Christian women in contemporary society, should be enough to establish that women were and are vital and normal parts of church leadership.

The Call of a Woman

Abraham left his homeland, Moses gave up wealth and political power in Pharaoh's court, and Peter left his fishing business. In addition to their giving up something that was important to them, each answered the call of God to follow Him completely. None had much idea what that would mean, but each demonstrated a willingness to sacrifice the known for the unknown because the call somehow touched him at the deepest level of his being.

God calls us as women to be mothers, nurturing life in every setting in which He places us. We are called to be life bearers in our homes, our communities, our churches, our schools, and our workplaces. Yet, in Genesis 3:16, we read, "I will greatly increase your pains in childbearing; with pain you will give birth to children." It could be physical or spiritual pain. For a woman to bring life into a situation she has to face her own vulnerability, rejection, and emotional pain.

When God called me into the ministry to play a very special and important role, I was afraid, scared, and shy. I wondered what people would say of me. How could Edith of yesterday become a leader or preacher of the Word? At first, it wasn't easy.

I see most speakers stand in front of a group and entertain or educate with boldness. But my calling as a woman is to bring forth or transform life. I can only do this if I am prepared to come out of hiding, abandon the mask, and be real and ready to face challenges that come my way with prayers and supplication unto God.

We bring life in a variety of ways—through a smile, a caring act, a kind word, wise insight that brings light into the darkest situation, through courageous challenge and sacrificial giving. All allow the life of Jesus to be clothed in our lives.

The call of God gives the power, courage, and boldness to confront the enemies. Esther was a great woman of courage, and God worked with and through her when she answered His call. Deborah was a judge and prophetess. She answered the call of God to deliver the children of Israel.

Many women are not standing in their places of calling because of fear. The call of God upon you is not because you are a rich woman or based on your social status, and so on.

You don't have to be a pastor to serve God. There are many ways to serve God, including a help ministry, teaching, evangelism, and ushering or performing other duties during services.

Responding to the call of God is what makes a beautiful life. And fulfilling the call of God is what makes a glorious life.

Sarah had a call from God. Her call was to give the promised child, to be the mother of many nations. She tried to manipulate in order to sell her gift. A woman who runs ahead of God, as Sarah did, invariably ends in more stress on the human personality than it can bear. Without a doubt, her biggest wrong was in her refusal to wait for God to work out His plan. We should always allow God to lead us and accomplish His purpose in our lives.

Hannah was called for a purpose. Israel needed a prophet, and God used Hannah to produce Samuel.

Every woman has a task in life. And you must have a place to hide, and that place is God. You cannot succeed without God. You have to tap into the place of God through prayer.

Jesus was moved by compassion when He saw the people dying. A good woman must have compassion for the people and work of God. God calls us to have a servant heart. You cannot serve God with a heart of stone.

Obedience and quality service is what God is looking for in the life of a good and divine woman. Before you begin to work as a minister of God, you must be sure of God's call on your life. Women should be actively involved in the Lord's vineyard. They can play effective roles in evangelism (especially child and youth evangelism); teaching foundational and Sunday school classes; participating in welfare or humanitarian services, such as visiting motherless babies, hospital ministry, prison ministry, providing for the poor and less privileged, and so on. In the Redeemed Christian Church of God, women can serve as pastors or assistant pastors. Make yourself available, and God will use you greatly.

In our society today and all over the world, it is a fact that women are more receptive to the things of God. They form the majority at prayer meetings, church attendance, conferences, and crusades.

A woman needs the spirit of God to help her work out her submission, spirituality, and strength of character. And when we look at God's divine role for women, as seen in Genesis 1:28, we find God faithfully helping her perform this role.

Women are to be completely set apart from God. They are to show loyalty and fondness to God. A true woman of God rests in amid any difficulty because she has discovered the magnificent work of God.

What about the contemporary women of faith, like Maria Woodworth Etter, Aimee Semple McPherson, Kathryn Kuhlman, and Mary Slessor. As they did exploits for God, these women suffered for the work of God. But despite the tribulation, humiliation, and rejection they encountered, they stood firm for the work of God. They were divine vessels in the hand of God.

Problems

Many women remain passive in the church. They are ignorant of their roles as mothers in their respective homes and as members in their churches.

In the church, many women are not involved in any activities. They come to sing and pray, and at the end of the service, they go home. They give less attention to the work of God in the church. Some of them are good at finding faults rather than facts. Some dodge responsibilities in the church with flimsy excuses. Many look unto man instead of Christ, the author and finisher of our faith. And at the end, they are disappointed and discouraged.

When they have given their lives to Christ, man and woman are regenerated and have equal opportunities to do exploits for God. Scriptures show that a woman can lead, be strong, and assert authority. The time has passed when women stay passive in the church without making any contributions.

Some women with great anointing have fallen by the wayside, thereby stagnating their calling. A lot of women have the anointing to be leaders, intercessors, teachers, evangelists, giants in the ministry of healing, or to share divine wisdom and to care and help others. Yet, with all these, are not effective in their homes. Why? Our homes are the baselines of our successes in any area. Why are we then not as effective as we should be?

Many women are no longer in submission to their husbands or to the leadership in churches. They do not show respect for their husbands and the church elders. Because of this, many women have destroyed their husbands' ministries and their callings. Many of us wear out our husbands with our complaints and nagging attitudes. This should not be so. Your husband is a special gift from God.

He was given to you to enrich your life. You are his helpmeet. If you keep complaining and grumbling, how can you fulfill your role as the helpmeet? Why don't you begin to appreciate him for who he is? If you want to enjoy your home, you have to submit to his godly authority, and stop all the murmuring and complaining. Our husbands need our help, support, and encouragement in all things they do. Divine women are submissive to their husbands (1 Peter 3:5).

The key lesson to be learned is the importance of the ministry of encouragement in the body of Christ. If there is a time in history when brethren need to be encouraged to patiently run the race set before them, it is today. There is so much discouragement, antagonism, poverty, and satanic activities against the church that make some, especially women, to lose hope and interest in the things of God. They may even backslide.

Women are often intimidated and not allowed to realize their God-given roles in the family, church, and society. They are regarded and treated as being inferior to their male counterparts and relegated to the background.

The fact that a woman is spiritually gifted does not mean she does not experience the needs of a normal woman. A woman needs to cope with fatigue, disillusionment, anger, depression, rejection, fear, poverty, loneliness, boredom, abuse, and envy.

Women should be encouraged in love, in faith, and in service. The character and work of Dorcas is typical of the influence of Christianity in the world, differentiating it from all other religious in caring for the weak and poor, lifting up women, and encouraging the weary-minded.

Dorcas was a true yoke bearer, demonstrating the true power of Christ, which always seeks to minister to others. She was a daughter of encouragement to the saints of God, and her works proved her faith in the Lord.

The task is not easy, but neither is it impossible. Today's woman must realize that trying to live on her own terms and by her own strength does not work. When we go the way of the flesh and rely on our strengths, we are more likely to wear out before our times.

A woman must submit herself to God and trust Him for the ability to live with her biological femininity and her cultural roles as well as the strong biblical distinctions between a man and a woman. Women should learn, know, and appreciate their positions in the inclusive plan of God for humankind.

Some denominations assert a woman's right to serve and teach but maintain she cannot be ordained. To "ordain" a person for service is to simply give the stamp of approval on one's life and ministry, and to support the person's response to God's call. Paul certainly stood behind the ministries of women and approved of their call by God.

In spite of this, the roles that require ordination (pastors, elders, and deacons) have traditionally been denied to women in many churches. In some circles, the teaching of men by women is not permitted, although ordination is not relevant here.

Some churches will tell you that apostle Paul instructs that women should not teach at all; rather, they are to remain silent in the church (1 Corinthians 14:34-35). This entire chapter of 1 Corinthians is focused on the importance of bringing peace and order among the people of Corinth. There was confusion due to the disruptive practice of people speaking at the same time. This was particularly a problem with some of those speaking in tongues. Women were not formally educated in anything and were even intentionally isolated at home to take care of the needs of their husbands and families.

First Corinthians 11 also shows that Paul assumes that women will both pray and prophesy in the church but should cover their heads when doing that.

To say that a woman cannot be ordained for the ministry is to deny her calling and to assert that God cannot, in His sovereign will, choose to call a woman to a certain ministry. God bestows His gifts as He chooses, and it is not always in accordance with what we expect.

Women do not have equal value with men but different roles in the family and church. The roles or the ministry to which one is called is determined by God's call to us individually, not one's gender.

Galatians 3:28 says, "there is neither Jew nor Greek, there is neither slave nor free, there is neither male nor female; for you are all one in Christ Jesus."

The husband is not accountable to God for the spirituality of his wife: "Every person will give account of himself/herself to God" (Romans 14:12).

In conclusion, we can say that there is no sanction in scripture for women to take roles of leadership, public ministry, and teaching. More important, if women are not allowed to have a voice or some kind of input, the church could be losing valuable resources. If a husband does not consider his wife's thoughts and ideas as important or valid, his family is surely incomplete, dysfunctional, and doomed to failure. Therefore, as the church strives to realize God's purpose for women, we must remember the truths of the scripture and apply them to our present-day culture. This allows men and women to present the Christian message to our world in the most powerful way.

Conclusion

Women have always been very important in God's plan and program for the world. Right from the beginning, God made women stand out as the last and the most excellent work of His creation. Women were the main support of Jesus's ministry. This certainly covers the gifts of help and administration, as well as other gifts (Matthew 27:55; Mark 15:41; Luke 8:3).

The woman was originally made by God in His image from one of Adam's ribs to be a helpmeet and for the glory of man (1 Corinthians 11:7–9).

God made woman for a specific purpose. He made her a helper to temper the man. That is the background of the saying, "Behind every successful man is a woman."

Women were last at the cross and the first to see and talk to the risen Lord (Matthew 28:8; Luke 24:5).

The scriptures are replete with great women of faith, some of whom are among the, "so great cloud of witnesses," that compass about us today. These women were good examples of the believers in word, in lifestyle, in love, in faith, and in service.

God wants to raise up women who understand that they have a role to play in His kingdom. Some women hide behind their husbands or undermine their ministries. But God wants women to be fully involved in His work. They could have ministries of their own. That could be evangelism ministry or intercessory prayer ministry, ministering to the less privileged, and so on. It is unfortunate when these divine key roles are abandoned, and a large percentage of gossipers, backbiters, lazy bores, busybodies, and so on is found among women.

Women should be encouraged to know who they are in the Lord, family, church, and the world at large. The examples of women in the Bible can help modern women everywhere to get stimulating and satisfying perspectives on their personal lives.

These are some important questions that need to be answered by every regenerated woman.

What is God's purpose for your life?

Do you know where your divine deposit should be channeled?

Are you wrongly channeled?

In every woman's heart there is a spark of heavenly fire that may lie dormant unless it is rightly positioned. Are you rightly positioned?

What contribution(s) have you made or are making in the ministry?

BIBLIOGRAPHY

Dr Ida Scudder *American physician and missionary who founded the Christian Medical College and Hospital in Vellore*

Wilson, Dorothy Clarke. *Dr. Ida: The Story of Dr. Ida Scudder of Vellore.* NY: McGraw-Hill, 1959.

Jeffery, Mary Pauline. *Ida S. Scudder of Vellore: The Life Story of Ida Sophia Scudder.* Mysore City, India: Wesley Press, 1951.

Eugenia Price. *God Speaks to Women Today (USA edition)* Zondervan 1973.

Teresa Kindred Bell. *Mom PHD. Howard Books* (December 1, 2004)

Warren W. Wiersbe. The Bumps Are What You Climb On. (2006)

Harriet Bicksler, & Kenton Brubaker. *Called to Stewardship.*

The Glorious Woman magazine (Mountain of Fire and Miracle Ministries)

www.ingramcontent.com/pod-product-compliance
Lightning Source LLC
LaVergne TN
LVHW042247070526
838201LV00089B/59